Also by Kevin Grant

Josyf Cardinal Slipyj, 1892-1984,
An Imitation of Christ.
Kirche in Not/Ostpriesterhilfe
Königstein, Germany
March 1985

Also published in French, German, Dutch,
Italian, Spanish and Ukrainian.

The Valiant Shepherd,
József Mindszenty 1892-1975.
Kirche in Not/Ostpriesterhilfe
Königstein, Germany
July 1986

Also published in French, German, Dutch,
Italian, and Spanish.

Kevin Grant

To Ann
Kindest wishes
Kevin
16 Oct 07

Deeps and Shallows

Verse captions to a minor life

Illustrations by Jake Grant

WORDS
Ink.

First published in 2007 by
Words Ink
PO Box 2001
Petworth
GU28 9YA

British Library Cataloguing in Publication Data.
A catalogue record for this book is available
from the British Library.

ISBN: 978-0-9529352-1-6

All Trade Marks are acknowledged.

Cover Design: Newline Graphics.
Photograph of Maureen: Photo-Mayo, Newcastle-upon-Tyne.
Photograph of Kevin, Thomas Bickerton; of Jake, Vincent Grant.

Book design and typesetting by Newline Graphics.
Typeset in ITC Stone Serif and Bembo.

Produced in Great Britain by
Jigsaw Print Productions Limited.

Distributors: Prompt Reply, PO Box 2001, Petworth
West Sussex GU28 9YA

For Maureen

Maureen, 1934-2004, in 1969.

Acknowledgements

I am indebted to numbers of people who have helped and encouraged me in the preparation of this collection. My friend Jon Wynne-Tyson, a true man of books and of letters, helped me in the selection and arrangement of the poems, his cautions being as prized as his affirmations. Other friends, Richard France, Rozanne Evans, John Eldridge, Frances Tait, Beryl Smyter and my son James also suggested corrections, refinements and improvements that I was grateful to receive and act upon.

Beryl, staunch lifelong friend of my late wife, Maureen, also drew in wise comments from her fellow members of Sidmouth Poetry Readers, Joyce Waterhouse, Dr Stewart Gordon, David and Dilys Blakeley-Belcher. Fr Robert Fintan Pollock, OP, Shirley Tull and my niece and god-daughter Annamarie Desmond gave me valued incidental guidance.

I am grateful to Tom Bickerton, my design consultant for 25 years, who typeset and designed my book with his customary limitless dedication and to Stephen Hajnal-Smith who eagerly assumed all print and production cares.

It is right also to thank my parents, Edward and Eileen Grant, he ever a poet, she always his muse, who affirmed and encouraged me when I was young. I have a record of some of my early poems only because my mother copied them out and saved them for me.

In expressing my gratitude to all these people I firmly take upon myself all residual shortcomings.

Titles in italic, in the contents and in the text, are lyrics,
to music by myself or others.

KG

Contents

Jurassic Port

As It Was, As It Is

Nursery Versery

In Grey Pavilion

Preface

I do not often trouble the public. The last time it happened, in 1973, it was an accident. For more about that curious incident see *The People who Read the Papers*, the prose envoi to the first section of poems here, *Thumbprints in the Archives*, on page 27. I am now back again, after a third of a century, this time imposing by design on the reader's patience. It is my modest hope to lodge a line or two in the public imagination for a second time.

A poet may not, in a preface, attempt an 'apologia pro carminibus suis', to baulk his critics. But a word or two of explanation may be in order. I have done this here and there throughout the collection but I make one general point here. Many of these verses are short, sometimes hardly verses at all. For me poems are like jokes, captions, headlines. When they are over, I stop. More than one person has said to me: "I never read long poems," a cultural change to which I have instinctively responded. Not many of these poems make it to a second page, only two to a third.

The engaging and firm-lined illustrations by my nephew Jake were all drawn working from the verses but it often and pleasingly seems that my lines are merely their captions.

My comments or satires on events over the years are under *Thumbprints in the Archives*, with my mentioned newspaper readership commentary of 1973 and its ensuing saga as their natural prose sequel.

Next I present my more sober items under *Unintended Baggage*, the prose exit piece here recalling the birth of our son, first published in *The Journal* (Newcastle).

The largest section, *Jurassic Port*, is the lightweight bravura department. There are restaurant napkins all over the place with rhymes I wrote, and gave away, and never saw again, a circumstance by which the reader may have been spared much. I include my previously unpublished conclave fantasy as the prose quota here.

As It Was, As It Is collects my religious verse. Many notabilities quickly establish in articles and interviews that they were brought up as Catholic but soon put all that behind them. Lapsed Catholic is indeed a big religion. Myself a creedal, cradle Catholic I am fine about that since the last line of my creed is the right of others to their creeds, or to none, or, indeed, to change their creeds on Wednesdays and Saturdays if they find that convenient. In July 1985 I received, in a dream, nothing mystical, just a dream, the words: "What is lost to Rome is not lost to God". My prose addition here, my advice to a son, took 14 years to assemble and write.

The *Nursery Versery* is drawn mainly from my unpublished 1977 collection, *Instant Rhymes for James*. My forbearing son has set no bar on my reproducing any of these. There are rhymes for other children as well. James asked me to include the Creed I wrote for him at that time, now pruned to the original 100-word target. I did not quite manage this compression at the time. It is almost verse in cadence but it goes here for the prose element.

Hardly fitting in anywhere else are short sport snippets, *In Grey Pavilion*. My own farewell to cricket, also written for *The Journal* (Newcastle), rounds this out but I can happily relate that I returned to the game in my early 40s with Gordon Brunton's 'Thomson Tycoons', playing a little better and drinking long pints with good men afterwards.

It is right to make clear that none of the cardinals in my conclave is based on any real cardinal, with us or gone before us. Other entirely fictional characters in these verses are Emma Leaven, Enid, Chloë, Ada Fradd and Decibel Jezabel.

Finally, I have nothing against any of the towns and other places that feature, all wonderful in their own way, I am quite sure. Some only appear because they rhyme nicely. I myself was born in modest Sidcup, Surbiton of the East, not a bad place to come from if you can't come from anywhere else.

Kevin Grant
October 2007

"Good heavens, a mobile!"

Thumbprints in the Archives

Afternoon thoughts in the South Library

3.00pm: After Napoleon

This wonder from the days of yore is
Iron-stepped and up two storeys
To epic tomes above, abundant,
Brass handrails curving up… redundant?
Great books, unvisited for ages,
Sages' unfrequented pages.
Dickens's relic Pickwick chair
Empty, just below the stair.
Gilded, cool, high, elegant,
Must this room end white elephant?
This dreamy chamber, lovely, rare,
Soon just a castle in the air?
All easier on screens below,
The newer, cruder means to know.

.../

4.30pm: After Earl Grey

Farewell, beloved library.
Hello, CD-Rom.
The once United Kingdom
united king dot com.
Onsets a bleaker winter yet,
The bloody, bloody Internet
With dismal triple w
To trip and trap and trouble you.
Ten billion "facts", at finger-click.
All true? Some? Which? I'm feeling sick.
"Help" and "Upgrades" make things worse,
Just steepening my learning curse.
Old tides wet-ankled King Canute,
New flows strand me as nincompute.

2007

Cat and Fiddle, '68

Humanae Vitae, France in a ferment,
Luther King shot, and Bob Kennedy.
No little dog laughed at Biafra's lament
Or at Czechoslovakia's threnody.
It wasn't the dish that forgot how to spoon,
It was Chi Chi and An An, the pandas,
And it wasn't the cow that jumped over the Moon,
It was Borman and Lovell and Anders.

1969

The Essex Girl

O, Emma, Emma Leaven,
O what a minx art thou,
Thy shoulder hard to cry on,
Cats-eyed beneath thy brow.

Hot harlot hard by Harlow,
In Woodford, pole-dance queen,
All men know whence thou'rt coming from,
All also where thou'st been.

No poor man's wish or thought could
Resist thy vamp veneer.
They're lost in Bishop's Stortford
Whenever thou draw'st near.

And many a fog-lost man said,
"She lured me ever faster."
Jet-setter's jinx at Stansted,
A mistress none can master.

Femme fatale in the fast lane,
Soft siren in the slow,
At Duxford flighty doxy,
Just how far wilt thou go?

"I'll strumpet up to Trumpington
Then *bas-bleu* on towards
Gowned Cambridge but don't go as far
As brazen Norfolk Broads."

2007

In Paperback

Oh, dear, what can the matter be?
Nothing to read except Lady Chatterley.
Mellors's the fellow that's all the rage latterly,
Connie's prolonged the affair.

1961

John Gone

Falling blossoms now delight us,
Nature's loveliest detritus,
Pink and white for us to glory at
As we mourn our Poet Laureate,
Feeling rather sad and numb and
Missing him whom bells have summoned.

1984

A Lady at Number Ten

Though they hatched up a putsch to dispatch her,
What stature in future for Thatcher.
  She loved argy-bargies,
   Routed Argies and Scargies,
No creature in nature could match her.

1999

Second Man

Should second man be reckoned an
Inevitable master?
Or does the heir, left too long there,
Succeed as a disaster?

Classify then all second men,
All deputies and vices.
I put to you, the types are two.
The first to be precise is

The happy breed who will succeed,
Whatever their profession,
To office, board, to crown or sword,
Whenever their succession.

Victoria's most glorious
Arrival on the throne
Assuaged the strains of earlier reigns,
Soon, half the world's her own.

George VI triumphed to fix the
Abdication's traumas
And Truman's tale – did he prevail! –
Is ever one to warm us.

.../

Grim Nazi crimes, then better times
For Germans – Adenauer.
Gaunt Charles de Gaulle found France her role,
Stood tall to guard her power.

But bring class two into review,
They weren't cut out to make it.
When their turn came they blew the game,
They simply couldn't take it.

Fate made this point to late anoint
The fumbling seventh Edward.
When Churchill went, poor Eden, spent,
Had reached the stage of deadwood.

Who now will laud pale pardoner Ford
Who white-washed wayward Nixon
Who, forcing fate, chose Watergate
To try his tacky tricks on?

The past is gone, so, moving on,
Consider current cases
This balanced verse will bless not curse
Those waiting for their places.

Dour Gordon Brown looked weighted down
Long waiting for appointment
But some new men at Number Ten
Have found flies in their ointment.

Prince Charles's prayer, "Lord, if you're there,
Let Mother live for ever."
By no means means that when The Queen's
No more he won't endeavour

To fill her place with equal grace
And prove that he's adepter
Than cynics fear in that sad year
When he accepts the sceptre.

Enough, it's time to end this rhyme
Of understudy rating.
Just one thing more, blind Milton saw,
They also serve while waiting.

1980/2007

Two Leaders

Macmillan fallen. Chaos. Feud. Thrombosis.
The new man, by political osmosis,
Admired, nobly sired, dapper, trim,
Sir Alec Home; but no one's heard of him.

Oh, what a contrast in New Delhi where you
Have only got, hear only Pandit Nehru.
They'd greet a *novus homo* ringing bells
But no one's heard of anybody else.

1963/2007

Yomping Song

Don't call the Falklands Malvinas
You know we will never let go.
They've always been a
Sore point between us
But they're not Malvinas
Or Argentina's.

1982

The people who read the papers

"Take what happened to Kevin Grant, for instance."

Words taken from Miles Kington's *Moreover* column in *The Times* of 20 January 1984. Miles was recounting how I, along with notables such as Bill Tidy and Jim Godbolt drew, wrote or said clever things which passed into general circulation with no credit or payment to their luckless originators.

I had a partner in oblivion, the late Brian Redhead. This was our tale. He wrote , in the long defunct *Adweek* magazine in April 1973, that *The Times* was read by the people who ran the country, *The Guardian* by the people who would like to. Next week they published a letter from me with a like epigram for each of the other papers:

The Financial Times is read by the people who run the country.

The Daily Telegraph is read by the people who remember how the country used to be.

The Daily Express is read by the people who think it is still like that.

The Daily Mail is read by the women who run the men who run the country.

The Daily Mirror (which once sought to run the country itself) is read by people who imagine they are running the country,

The Morning Star is read by people who want another country to run the country.

Meantime *The Sun* sounds its crumpet voluntary. Mr Murdoch has found a gap in the market. It is the oldest gap in the world.

I added that one day I'd tell them about the Sundays but their amorphous unparticularity has always defied my powers of epigram and I have never managed it.

I was briefly famous in about four pubs around Gray's Inn Road and struck up an enduring friendship with Brian. Then came the autumn and we were dazzled by a blaze of obscurity. Our lines were being quoted everywhere and were broadcast over and over – but never a mention of us.

Taking a vow of celebrity I began to fight back, getting letters into journals like *UK Press Gazette* staking our claim but then a book came out quoting the whole rigmarole, a bit garbled, on its dust jacket. Decently enough publisher Hutchinson paid us thirty quid. So did Hugh Hefner when he ran them in *Playboy*. Then came the big time. The late Dave Allen featured the lines in his show *Dave Allen at Large* on 18 October 1973. Again, no credit. I missed it but everyone rang me to tell me. The BBC behaved well and from then on cheques began to flow. Brian and I divided the light spoil on the old tax fraction of two-ninths to him, seven to me. Cash rarely changed hands, the benefits being paid in kind in good restaurants. The sums were sometimes trifling; "£4.00 for fourth showing in Zambia".

By now my *Sun* joke had been developed by someone closer to the street than I. It had become: "The people who read *The Sun* don't care who runs the country as long as she's got big tits!" This was Before Margaret so there was nothing personal. Meantime the jokes had received the people's accolade of circulation around shops, offices, factories, and loo doors. There was even a saucy postcard selling in a south western seaside resort with our stuff. I'd still like to get a copy of that.

Miles Kington takes up the tale. He rang Brian Redhead to check the facts – his only ever sortie, he says, into investigative journalism – and Brian told him my response to the later launch of the *Daily Star*. "The scriptures were wrong, Brian – there *is* something new under *The Sun*."

As time passed the jokes were used on tv by Dickie Henderson, Rory Bremner, Larry Grayson and others but their highest flight was when Jonathan Lynn and Sir Anthony Jay included them in an episode of *Yes, Prime Minister*. They were in the programme and in their follow-up book, *Yes, Prime Minister, the Diaries of the Right Hon James Hacker, Volume II*. They wrote their own excellent quip for the tyro *Independent*. "*The Independent* is read by people who don't know who runs the country but are sure they are doing it wrong". I never thought of anything for the mayfly *Today*, which was sad. It was a good effort.

When I let Jonathan and Anthony know that it was our stuff they were quick with congratulatory apology, and we got a cheque. A Downing Street official had slipped them the text as a bit of Civil Service folklore. In 1988 I fixed a lunch in my club with Brian and both of them, one of those perfect occasions that never quite seemed to end as we sank deeper into the afternoon and the armchairs. Miles, invited, pleaded that freelances could never come to London just for lunch but he would surely have added more to our day than he would have subtracted from his own. We missed him. And we can't go round again without Brian.

The last chapter is that BBC2 chose 'our' episode of *Yes, Prime Minister* as among the funniest in the series in its marathon search for the best ever sitcom. When they showed the number to telephone if you wanted to vote for *Yes, Prime Minister* it was the dear old newspaper jokes they flashed up. Thirty years on, goodness me.

Unintended Baggage

Cheat Heart

Sad man that's wanting faith and sense and duty,
You yearn for, woo, win, wed some trusting beauty
And when she's home, a loving wife and mother,
You weave new fantasies around some other.

1970

Deeps and Shallows

In the shallows of my eyes
You splashed and played
And passing pleasure found,

Whilst, in the deeps of yours,
I thrashed, afraid
And, at your leisure, drowned.

2000

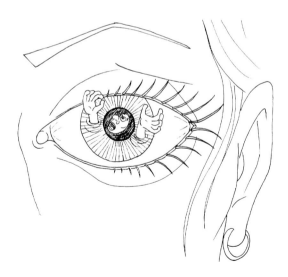

Eighth Decade

The prospect of the eighth decade
Finds this old idler low, dismayed.
The urgent muse, long disobeyed,
Those projects, dreams and tasks delayed
Now slip my grasp, I'm made afraid.
I tarried, parried that swift maid,
The calendar, that minx-most jade.
Her hand, light on young shoulder laid,
Now urgent, firm and heavy weighed.
She, curving scythe and scraping spade,
Long borrowed from, must now be paid,
As powers, hopes, delights, all fade.

2003

Enid

A frail and faded lady, she,
Her life just chores and cups of tea,
Anonymous, to you and me,
But known to God, loved tenderly.
Then, Saturday, at half-past three.

Young Jills jostling, send her flying,
Break her glasses, start her crying.
Young Jacks jeering, drunk from town,
Knock her down and break her crown
On Saturday, at half-past three.

But God who waits till Jacks and Jills
In turn grow old, bear their own ills,
Marks their deeds and lines their faces
With ineradicable traces
Of Saturday, at half-past three.

2007

Gin and Chronic

The juniper, the juniper
Has danced away with Chloë.
The berry's going to bury her,
Quick, quick, sloë, sloë.

2004

Mourning After

There's now a morning-after pill
To lull the night before.
But where's the after-mourning pill
To heal the heart left sore?

2006

October Cottage Pictured from the Sky

October Cottage pictured from the sky
Looks happy, waving white hands overhead.
Its old and twinkling eyes inspect the world
Above a nose the Black Boy's ales made red.

The yellow plaster's Norman's gift, the name.
Brown cows sedately star the fine green sky
And dinky toys from boxes all the same
Patrol the blue stripe road that's running by.

And on the parchment of the field below
A farmer's hand has written lines of worth.
They're mystery nursery rhymes; we only know
They speak the fruits and beauty of the earth.

*Norman Barrett, friend, musician and sign-writer,
painted the house name for us.*

1989

On Life's Ocean

Got some?
Risk flotsam.
Quit get some,
Join jetsam.

2007

On One of Her Last Birthdays

With great love from your old troubadour

Your heart is sometimes troubled now, I know,
By pangs of growing older, letting go.
I see the pensive look on your dear face
Recalling years gone by that you'd retrace.
All days, all years are good and equal blessed,
Though love's first days are sweet her last are best.

8th October

On the Death of my Maureen

I do. I will.
Shared Sacrament Divine,
Bone of my bone,
Two in one flesh; hers, mine.

But she, half flesh of mine,
Is laid in earth,
And I, now half my flesh,
Am half my worth.

2004

Remembrance Day

As the child felt it

Some of our fallen heroes
Are forgotten and unknown
While others have memorials
Of marble or of stone.

But every single soldier
Deserves our utmost praise,
So don't forget those heroes
On Remembrance Days.

Each soldier fallen in the war
Is a man we should remember,
So don't forget those gallant men
On the eleventh of November.

Each man that died for liberty,
Each man that died for peace
Was a man of boundless courage
For whom our prayers should never cease.

So sometimes think of those heroes
Who perished in the fray,
To save that same democracy
That we enjoy today.

1945

Second Gift

A white horse ambled up, a gift.
He stood so close, his muzzle warmed my hand.
I let him go. I didn't understand.
Then he came back, a second gift, beside me,
Eager, saddled, bridled, urging, "Ride me."
So now I've swung me up to prize
and ride him.
He walks, trots, canters,
gallops, me astride him.

2006

Seeing my Skull

Tired, tired on the Underground.
The red arc of the logo is a skull cap
On that dark, bald man's head,
For one moment a bishop.
And then, a moment on,
I see my own skull there,
In the dark, dark of the double window,
Laughing at me from in behind my face.

2004

A Star Looks in

The child again

Once way on high in a midnight sky
One star shone on its own.
A waiting cloud was its lovely shroud
As it hung there all alone.

Its gentle light in rippling flight
Chanced past a prison bar
Alighting on a woebegone
Who turned to watch the star.

But soon, alas, the cloudy mass
Came closing round all plainly.
His haven new slid out from view
And left him watching vainly.

1946

Straighten that Face

My father told me not to cry
But what he didn't say was why
I shouldn't cry. So I cried on.

Mother, passing, heard my wailing.
Seeing her made all plain sailing.
I dried my eyes, my crying done.

2007

Sunset Madrigal

I

"Twinkle, wrinkled fading star,
What you were's not what you are.
Once so high, up in the sky,
Now forgotten. Gone. Goodbye."

II

But as the Golden Oldie wept
A gallant ancient swift upleapt
"Ignore those cruel words. They're wrong.
I'll sing to you a fairer song.

"There's nothing young girls know or do
To match your magic. Stay, it's true.
Your grace, your knowing touch are far
Beyond pert gawks. You're still my star."

2001/ 2006

To Drama School

Seventeen, the perfect blessed age,
The world's before you
And the world's a stage.
Go with a light, sure step
Upon its boards.
Be generous –
And reap its true rewards.
One thing it asks
Of players great and small
Before it gives –
It asks of you your all.

1984

Twenty Daisies Foiled

Beware the man who daisies bears
For here's a man who really cares.
No Tesco bucket's snatched bouquet,
No afterthought, no by the way,
No mobile call to Interflora
From this impassioned new adorer.
Oh, no, he's knelt in morning dew
To pick them, one by one, for you.
Take care, dear madam, you can bet
His trouser knees got soaking wet.
He's rummaged for some chocolate foil,
And smoothed it out, a dainty toil.
Concede, sweet face, there's not a lot'll
Better signify besottal.
    And though his path's four-boulder strewn
      His heart moves to the oldest tune.
        These daisies might last all your life
          In loving, bound to him as wife.

Undated

Unintended Baggage

The passenger was dreaming
Through the window
Of lovely things.
But then the train,
Reproving his euphoria,
Announced its "Final station stop – Victoria,
Please take all your longings with you."

2004

When I Come Home

The other night I couldn't sleep,
I lay awake.
I couldn't sleep, I lay awake
And thought of you.

The other night I slept so well,
I dreamt a dream.
I slept so well, I dreamt a dream,
I dreamed of you.

The other night, Maureen, I woke,
I woke and sighed.
Maureen, I woke, I woke and sighed,
I sighed for you.

And now tonight I sleep and dream,
Rejoice and hold,
I sleep and dream, rejoice and hold
You close once more.

1977

Firstborn

The oldest tale and the newest tale. A little before midnight I set out with the dog for our constitutional mile. I returned to learn that on the stroke of midnight things had started. My wife protested that morning would do, but I had too long nursed my dread of amateur delivery in Gosforth High Street to allow any such hazard.

The Oxford is a fine car, admirably accoutred, but its equipment falls short of such calls. By 3 am, the classic obstetric hour, she was protesting but safe in hospital.

I began a book, a novel on the life and times of Thomas Chatterton. But three children were born in the prelude. I gave up. I spoke with another husband, capped, masked and gowned. His weary vigil was finishing. "It's a little girl," the nurse tells him. "Congratulations," I say. Then they sent me home. "Come back in the morning."

Having screwed up my courage in both hands (one would have done) I had applied to be present throughout. So before nine in the morning I was back, ludicrously obscured myself now in cap and mask and gown. "Men don't know they're born," they've always told me. As the hours pass I learn a little. Green as my gown I am kindly led away to lunch before two.

I never get back in. I sit giving glassy attention to an excellent Agatha Christie. The nurse is coming. I rise awkwardly. "You have a little boy." It is five-to-three on St Patrick's Day. He is ten days early – to make up for being ten years late.

Spreading the news

I rush to telephone the good news to London and Liverpool. James Patrick Newman is here, is well and is welcome. I thought his initials rather fine but a brother has written to say that he sounds like an extinct railway company.

He is James for the Epistle writer, whoever he was; scholars are unsure. Patrick for the Roman Celt who converted the country that is still converting the world. Newman is for the Cardinal. It expresses the instinctive affection of an English Catholic for the Anglican Church. He is a kindly light on unity's path.

The infant was baptised on Easter morning. His godfather, and uncle, is a Newcastle man. I declared he must follow his father and support Charlton Athletic, but his sponsor claims direction of his deeper allegiances; his team will be Newcastle. They play at St James's, after all.

It is agreed, nonetheless, that he follows Kent in the greater game. None of this summer defection to Yorkshire, so widely met with up here. A happy arrangement; football is, after all, simply a way of keeping the men fit in winter. As for Oxford and Cambridge, he will decide for himself, suddenly and irrevocably, as we all do the first time we understand the race.

Welcome, James, welcome. And while your mother gives you that bottle I must get Dunstan's collar round him. It is time for his walk.

This article first appeared in "The Journal",
Newcastle-upon-Tyne, on 12th April 1967.

Jurassic Port

Ada Fradd

This is the tale of Ada Fradd
Whose maiden name was Fuzzard.
She wrote a little, late, and bad,
Then died, at Leighton Buzzard.

1969

Air Engineer Cadet Nichamin

A tiddley-winks player called Nichamin
Was so skilled he'd no need to flick 'em in.
      He'd stand on the mat
      With one eye shut, like that,
And with RAF boots on he'd kick 'em in

1952

Avon Graffito

Ah, maiden, maiden, slumb'rest thou yet alone?
Squand'rest thou yet thy cheek upon
    some fortun'd pillow
When we might wedded be and prove thy dreams?

1972

Cloistered Avarice

There was a young nun from Dalrymple
Whose spiritual failure was simple.
        She was perfectly chaste
        And completely abased
But she hid forty quid in her wimple.

1969

Debtor Suitor

A certain lady's all my bliss
But also half my sorrow.
She never lets me steal a kiss
But sometimes lets me borrow.

My debt is mounting in a stack
To her whom I admire.
To pay, I have to kiss her back
And thus my dues go higher.

2006

Decibel Jezabel

A merciless alto from Billingshurst
Liked to sing every Sunday in thrilling bursts.
      Her rising cadenzas
      Were something tremendous
But she liked you to give her ten shillings first.

c 1986

Diana Muldoon

My young brother Michael said,
    "Kev, here's a tanner,
You're commissioned to write some fine verse,
    as a boon,
For the eightieth birthday of peerless Diana,
The noble four-score of the gentle Muldoon."

So a day or so on I sat down and began an
Assault on the task at a time opportune.
I found it no labour to muse on Diana,
That lady of sparkle, the laughing Muldoon.

One Irish endearment you'll hear is "Alanna",
A term the young blades whisper under the moon.
But the name that we whisper is simply "Diana"
For a flash of those eyes from the lovely Muldoon.

We are quickly beguiled by the charm of her manner
Be it morning or evening or late afternoon.
Any time is just fine to pass time with Diana
"Let me pour you a large one,"
    says hostess Muldoon.

So gather a crowd round the parlour pianna
Let's sing "Happy Birthday", the old happy tune.
Your arrivals are always too late, dear Diana
Your departures, by contrast, too soon,
    sweet Muldoon.

2002

Early on Friday Evening

Hair up,
Eyes down,
Precious to herself,
Sixteen.

1970s

Emotion Picture

He said, "Let me be your servant."
She said, "No, please be my friend."
But when he said, "Be my sweetheart."
She just smiled and sa-i-d,

THE END.

Undated

Epidemic Paratitis

A lousy thing to have benight us
Is epidemic paratitis.
I give this plague its formal style
Since common mumps sounds much more vile.
It adds the jibe of juvenility
To pain and threat of infertility.
When told about your swollen glands
Your friends all laugh and clap their hands.
"He'll get the measles in a bit."
"Or nappy rash," puts in a wit.
The sufferer swells and sweats and swears.
He's feeling low but no one cares.
So, if you want support, compassion
Select an illness more in fashion.

1964

G-G-Gently Let Him Go

I l-l-like you very much
Dear suitor, b-b-but
You haven't got the magic touch
I l-l-long for.

   CUT.

2006

Guess Inn Game

As I sip Guinness in this inn
My query, to begin is,
Is the Guinness in the inn
Or is the inn in Guinness?

2006

Hart and Buck Lock Antlers

Chorleywood
Is jolly good
But Chalfont St Giles
Is better, by miles.
Then, some aver that nowhere's sweeter
Than elegant Chalfont St Peter.
Whilst none here reckons it need yield
To overweening Beaconsfield.

2007

He Saw Three Ships

The Inspector of Wrecks at Wells-next-the-sea
Was depressed because there were no wrecks to see
      But one night a typhoon
      Left his foreshore bestrewn
With three ships, lifting him into ecstasy.

1980s

Headstone

I

Iambic pentameter
On a headstone
Looks amateur,
So can a sonnet
Chiselled on it.
Some, high up in IQ, like you,
Favour the seventeen-foot haiku
Whilst the dimmer pick
The limerick.
Classier, really, if they bury you
Below a clerihew.

II

Also, prose goes.

1995

Humberside, with Goxhill

The two 'Umberside verses are to be read in a
Yorkshire/North Lincs accent, if there be such.
The Goxhill verses revert to RP, Sidcup branch.

'Ere's terrible, of 'ope no glimmer,
'Ull is dull and Grimsby grimmer.
But, you'd 'ave to say that *the* corpse,
A mile from prom t't sea, is Cleethorpes
       – that town's a proper parcel.

On 'Umber Bridge's soaring spans
On foot, in cars, bikes, scores in vans,
'Ull Kingston Rovers' roaring fans
Fill up their 'eads with boring plans
       – and dreams of Barbara Castle.

But lift your head. Go see Goxhill
Where, close to nature, joy may still
Through happy creatures fully fill
By courtesy of Shirley, Bill,
       – a happier horizon.

For here's a horse of happy mien,
More years than hands, yet springeth green.
Though Hillie's now just semi-shod
He prances like a demi-god
       – a sight to feast your eyes on.

Dismantled cars, a chassis, bonnet
Close by the pond, with ducks upon it
In sundry colours, quacking, grazing,
White eggs in quantities amazing
     – I washed them; I've my uses.

Enhancing nature's alchemy
Above the pond, with balcony,
A timber summer-house of ease is
Set, from which each prospect pleases
     – a bower for the muses.

Go half a dozen strides up higher,
Find timbered frames of chicken wire,
A coop asquawk with black-red hens
Though lazy layers, these denizens
     – Bill's fencing thwarts the foxes.

But now, for more, please come inside.
Where reigning cats and dogs abide.
Ginger Rodney, huge, likes sleeping.
Black Fidget, she-cat, loves a leaping
     – on tables, chairs, in boxes.

.../

Five dogs ensure a constant bustle
Retrievers, Labradors, Jack Russell.
The Golden boys are Kingsley, Bracken,
Control of these two mustn't slacken
        – some rooms are out of bounds.

Digby's the old black Labrador,
Arthritic, lame, he romps no more.
With half his wit and twice his blarney
Runs in, crash, bang, the wild brown Barney
        – the strongest of five hounds.

Half blind, half deaf, slow, very small
Rules nipper Rupert, feared by all.
Is he Bill's dog? You'd think this true but
Bill, in fact, belongs to Rupert
        – the artful little dodger.

In loose command of all this life
Dwell Bill and Shirley, man and wife,
Who, by the by, do B & B,
A miracle, it seems to me
        – their passing, grateful lodger.

2006

I Am Who I Am

I am who I am,
Whoever that is,
Whoever that happens to be,
And this is today,
Whenever that is,
And they tell me it's quarter-to-three.

1970

In the Restaurant

Sweet waitress, come,
Remove this muck.
We ordered yum,
You brought us yuk.

1979

In the Shower

Better, unfathomably, in a northern accent.

Years ago somebody told us,
"Wash your 'air with 'ead & shoulders."
So, when I shower, that's what I do.
But I don't just use it as shampoo.
I use it like a shower gel
To wash the rest of me, as well.

I know that might seem strange,
    to some;
      But I've not got dandruff
        on me bum.

2000

In his Place

He said, "Are you good in bed?"
She said, "No, I'm good. Instead."

2006

Jurassic Port

It seems Tyrannosaurus Rex
Preferred the booze to having sex.
There really can be little doubt,
This preference helped to wipe him out.

2006

The Lady Kantankera Morning Frown

The Lady Kantankera Morning Frown
Comes pouting and frowning and yawning down.
"Make me some tea
Immediately,"
Or the dressing-gowned one gives a dressing down.

2006

Lintas House
- In for a Penny

What cruel deceiver chaos sought,
And made our lives with hazard fraught?
Who was it, I shall hedge no more,
Transposed the loos from floor to floor?

Eighth floor, north end, the matter's clear,
Facilities for ladies here.
But on the seventh, girls, take care,
To boxes stalls are added there.

Go down to six and see once more
The legend "Ladies" on the door.
One floor below, I'm glad to say
The gentlemen again hold sway.

But steady, brother, one floor down,
They haven't knocked the whatsits down.
Those basins aren't there to annoy –
You're in the ladies' loo, old boy!

Press on, we beg, the third floor's near
You'll find things there don't look so queer.
By now a law may seem emergent
That makes this contretemps less urgent.

.../

North loos to girls on even floors,
On odd, find "Men" upon the doors.
But trusting girls who think this true
Should watch their step when on floor two.

Down there the rule makes its exception –
Girls get a very odd reception!
Descend once more dear ladies and
You'll find the fort by ladies manned.

And on the ground again they score
So overall they win, 5-4.
Which probably is only fair
Since they're inclined to linger there.

Enquiries show that lack of caution
Has led a fairly high proportion
Of the staff in this to blunder.
What's the remedy, we wonder?

Pink doors and blue is one suggestion
That might abate this cruel congestion.
Or else, on every door have fixed
Not "Men", not "Ladies", no – just "Mixed".

c 1963

Listen, Mya Sunshine

The English believe that 'O Sole Mio' is a love song.
Alas, not so. The literal meaning of the title is 'Listen,
Sunshine.' It is a warning from the Mafia. A fearless
Italian waiter cracked the Neapolitan code for me,
in New York. I scribbled down his broken English on
my table napkin.

Listen, mya sunshine,
Don'ta gif me trouble
Or I come sometime
And your 'ousa be rubble.

You treata me crappily,
I tella my friends from Napoli.
They pronto come and smasha
Youra face quite 'appily.

Mario, Padrino from Sicily,
'E finda you verra easily,
'E changea you physically,
'E senda da boys in;
Your cappuccino poison.
You listen good, my sunshine.

You thinka I'ma joking,
Is a big mistaka.
My gun soona be smoking
Fromma my Studebaker.

.../

At noon you pulla da fast one,
Gonna be your last one,
We burn your ice-cream carta
Befora 'arf-past one.

Ma, -a-a-a-a, a-a-a-a -rio, Padrino from Sicilia,
With heem you don'ta wanta getta familiar.
'E don't mind if 'e kill ya.
'E come to see ya.
'E bomb your trattoria.
So listen good,
My sunnashine.

2000

The Little Match Girl

Gilda
Strikes men like matches.
Holds them fast in her pearl-topped,
Soft pink clutches,
Lets them curl and blacken.
But just before the heat
Can scorch her own exquisite flesh
Drops them at her feet.

Sometimes she grinds these embers
Beneath her cool stiletto,
Smiles, and remembers.
Revenge for Rigoletto.

2000

The Milliner's Song

Now here's a truth, my friends, I swear,
There never was a face so fair
That wasn't prettier, I vow,
With bonnet set upon its brow.

2007

Oh, I Say, Look Here!

A dodgy countess from Turin
Liked to sin if you plied her with gin.
     So, what I did next
     Was, I sent her this text:
"If the count's going out, count me in!"

2006

On the Underground

Lower fares, fewer stairs, 'phone repairs
      – main entreaty.

Bouncy pairs, cheeky stares, unawares
      – what a pity.

Student airs, law despairs, no one cares
      – penny ditty.

French au pair's dress that dares, loud "Oh, yeahs"
      – my, she's pretty!

Bookstall wares, stocks and shares, pinstripe glares
      – in the city.

Love affairs, surely there's hope she cares
      – *more* graffiti!

1977

Quango

Why, when it takes but two to tango
Are seventeen required to quango?

2004

Reflection

(This is not a fits-all-sizes verse. Readers are encouraged to bespeak the last two lines according to their own condition.)

Mirror, mirror on the wall
I don't look like that at all.
I am lean, bronzed, fine and fit,
Not a puny, paunchy git.

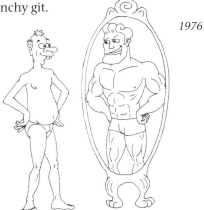

1976

Sadness, Sadness by the Sea

Marry in Hastings,
Repent at St Leonards.

c 1998

Seven Deadly Virtues

This poem was written as an entry to a "Spectator"
competition. It was not among those chosen for
publication, all of which were better, in my view and
the view of the judges, than this. But I like it well enough
to include it, just.

Set **candour** first, its rapier thrusts few
    human hearts defend.
"Save, oh, save me," Canning pleaded,
    "from the candid friend."

Next up is **punctuality**, this courtesy of kings
It's only so when it's observed; imposed it's
    barbed, and stings.

Third, **niceness**. Let's be loved by all,
    complacently abide.
If what's in front, well, isn't nice, pass on
    the other side.

Hindsight the moving finger stays,
    amender in arrears,
Makes clock-hands anti-clockwise fly and
    spares us all our tears.

.../

To deadly **charm**, my next alarm, charism less the is,
Attraction less the action, less likely hers than his.

Praise prudence, driven well by love, you're less if
    you have missed her.
But flee grey **caution**, fuelled by fear,
    her miserable sister.

Last, grim **PC**, correctitude. In Hell, I am not joking,
A notice says: "Burn as you please, but thank you for
    not smoking."

2006

Sigma Enigma

The sigma sign means add, not multiply,
The sign should help, it should not stultify.
Will you please give me the result if I
Call out the sigma sign?

1960

Speak only Good of the Dead

De mortuis nil nisi bonum
Is a load of old phonum-balonum.
> Our bones are not cold
> When the dark tales are told
And there's no coming back to disown 'em.

2005

There's no Arguing about Tastes

De gustibus non disputandum,
To pluck one more saying at random,
> Displays the great strength
> That examined at length
You can say it's been taken in tandem.

2005

A Tremor Fore

Soft cheeks, soft eyes,
Two softer lips,
A waist to prize,
Curved, swaying hips.

A judder aft,
A tremor fore,
All mothercraft's
Sweet semaphore.

1982 and 2007

The Virus

"They magnify us with their microscopes,
The dopes.
I wonder why they so admire us?"
Thought the virus.

1964

What am I?

I'm slim and black
And bent of back,
My face is orange fire.
My wings are two,
The lower blue,
Whilst yellow soars the higher.

The answer to this riddle in on page 112.

2004

Another Conclave

In 2005 the world's media crowded into Rome, fascinated by the best horse-race in history's sporting calendar, a conclave to elect a pope. The cardinals, all eminent, some prominent, circled the Square in St Peter's in huddles and clusters, soon to be locked out of the Italian sunshine and into the Sistine Chapel. They would not be let out until they'd chosen a pope, a man charged with squaring the circle, with aligning earth's moral geometry with that of heaven.

But yield to fancy; forget the real conclave for a moment. Imagine another one, in which all the hopes and fears of the faithful found embodiment in particular candidates. Who *might* have been there? Who *might* have slouched in awkward cassock to the balcony? The candidates varied in prospect from *persona papabilis* and *persona grata* to *persona ignota* and *persona getlosta*.

Cardinal Anticristo Charming and popular. Present at every conclave. He doesn't always know who he is. He is usually identified and stopped. But one day he might not be.

Cardinal Ardac du Foleau A cultured polymath, this humble Frenchman was thought to have been too much in awe of the late Pope.

Cardinal Crunch The only serious candidate from the British Isles. Wanted to smack down on dissent. Favoured a leaner, smaller, disappearing Church. Would have made women wear hats at Mass again.

Cardinal Doneromein Very, very tired and sought a quiet life in Rome away from his chaotic US archdiocese.

.../

Cardinal Dumpadalumba Would have closed down the Vatican and run the papacy from his African archdiocese. Greatly feared in the Curia. In cahoots with Sitsvac (qv).

Cardinal Duslipsunagulli The communications expert from the subcontinent. A master of spin. Knew Cowdrey and Mountbatten. A safe pair of hands. Possibly several safe pairs.

Cardinal Gensec This Slav curialist survived the Communist era. Strong centralist and master of bureaucracy. Very popular in the trattorias. A heavy smoker and genius at chess and poker.

Patriarch Hivaidski Popularly known as "The Man from the Stans". Philosopher, canon lawyer, medical doctor, diplomat, and mystic, he had been a professional footballer before entering the priesthood.

Cardinal Iffibutti Was not really sure whether he wanted the job or was up to it or what he would have done if elected. Was a very strong candidate.

Cardinal Kondomoke This North American Indian was thought too progressive by some but was popular in sub-Saharan Africa. A Harvard man who made it in oil before becoming a priest, and a personal chum of Hivaidski.

Cardinal Lagervoucher German lawyer and social reformer. Was almost certainly the 'Bumpsidaisy' of the famous *Hans Kung und Bumsidaisy* knock-about theology duo who teased the Church in the 'eighties with their daring essays. Way, way out but might have got in.

Cardinal Maipoloancora An immensely disagreeable old curialist greatly troubled by the personal style of the late Pope.

Cardinal Sedevacante Loves conclaves and was set to delay white smoke with cunning and vigour. Was determined to do nothing at all if elected. He was a real danger.

Cardinal Sitsvac East European who'd have sacked the entire Curia, especially Gensec, and started again. The only candidate with a minder and a taster. Seen around a lot with Dumpadalumba.

Cardinal Trendilefti A dangerous South American and a supporter of Tottenham Hotspur. Could have run hot after a ninth or tenth vote when the cardinals start getting fed up.

Cardinal U Cant Enigmatic Burmese. Would have been more a binder than a loosener as popes go. Crony of Crunch.

Cardinal Udleikavodka Charming and sociable Balkan. Ordained secretly under Communism. For years an *in petticoato* member of the Sacred College. The only woman candidate. Jested she'd have been Joan II if elected.

Cardinal Van Inagen Egregious Dutchman who made his name as a Wimbledon qualifier in the 'sixties. Hadn't done much since.

Cardinal Van Outagen Van Inagen's life-time rival. Good in eleventh-hour scenarios. Could well have been the man.

As It Was,
As It Is

As It Is

O Lord, make me not rich, famous or powerful,
I am doing enough harm as it is.

c 1970

Backwards and Forwards

Follow the rule of Saint Francis
In any temptation you meet.
If you're making improper advances
Perhaps you should go on retreat.

2001

Christmas Stocking Song
for Maureen

This, with its music, was our Christmas card that year.

Christmas log smoke billows forth,
Can't choose east, west, south or north.
Wind don't know which way to blow.
Smoke don't know which way to go.
The wind won't blow and the smoke won't go.

Christmas goose fat smoking rare,
Kitchen smothered, got no air,
Smoke don't know which way to go,
The wind won't blow and the smoke won't go,
Jubilate Domino.

1998

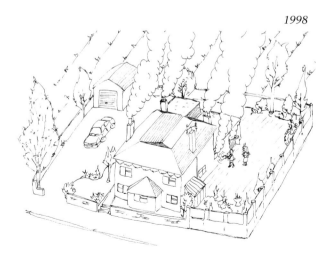

Don't Keep Looking at your Watches

Next time you're asked, "How old are you?"
Reply like this: "My staff is new,
I take great care to cut no notches.

"This life's a banquet, tickets free,
Why show its Host discourtesy
By always looking at our watches?"

2007

An End to all our Waiting

*I had been asked to sing 'Holy Night' at Midnight Mass
in 1992. At rehearsal a day or so earlier we realised that
the one verse we had was not long enough for the
liturgical space allotted. So I wrote this new verse.
It is sung first because that's where its idea fits in the
Christmas narrative.*

O, Holy night, an end to all our waiting,
It is the night that the maid bore a son.
God's will fulfilled, all earthly grief abating,
Bow down your heads, worship God's Holy One.
The trumpets sound with angel chorus mingling
While shepherds haste to greet the wondrous child.
Kneel there with them, be still before the mystery,
The world's Saving Light in a manger gently laid.
O night divine, holy night, night divine.

1992

The Facts of Life

When we were young the facts of life
Were things our mothers told us.
They told us late, we had to wait,
No old heads on young shoulders.

But now ungodful fervour brings
Dark facts too soon from others.
These dismal facts of life are things
The young daren't tell their mothers.

2007

Finger Rosary

*Upon considering a finger rosary as a sword beaten into a
circle, its handle now the Cross.*

You are the circling of the sword.
When we wear this ring we are yours in prayer.
You are where we bring what we cannot bear.
　　　　You are the Mother of the Word.

1978/ 2006

How Will it Be to Die?

How will it be to die?
One day I'll know
And leave all living men
To wonder still,
How will it be?

1970

Looking at our Son

The griefs and doubts,
The care and sin,
No era to
Be parents in.

Two trusting eyes,
One joyful smile,
Yes, little son,
It is worthwhile.

c 1967

Lourdes: The Miracle of the Bells

Brother Walgan Francis, FSC, is long years with God but he always knew how to temper piety with mercy. This is a true story; the priest, of unquestionable fervour, was attempting a second sermon after a long Mass before the Grotto on a cold day.

To stop that sermon Brother Walgan
Didn't simply use an organ.
As history avows and tells
The man preferred a thousand bells.

The first words of the priest's oration
Set off the tintinnabulation.
The Sanctuary and Domain
Though wide and great could not contain
The thunder of that carillon
That filled them both and still tolled on
Its clangour rousing town and suburb,
None escaped the fearful hubbub
Rolling over hill and valley,
The sermon-smashing great reveille
Set each breast with wonder throbbing,
The very cable-cars went bobbing.

The priest gave up. A strained "Amen."
The bells stopped too. Peace reigned again.
Despising earthly means – I'm lyrical –
Brother Walgan worked this miracle.

1985

Love's Answer

I was doubt, asking, "Can I trust you?"
I was night, denying your day.
I was death, saying, "Now I've lost you."
I was pride saying, "I'll go away."

You were faith, saying, "Now, believe me."
You were day, saying, "Now, awake."
You were life, saying, "Come and live me."
You were love, saying "Give…and take."

1977

New Limbo

I

A sinner died, aged eighty-two,
A happy thing for him to do.
Or so it seemed, for he'd been poor,
Worn out, alone, unwell, no cure.
But he'd long quit the godly leaven
So trembled at the gate of heaven.
St Peter, with St Elutherius
– they work in pairs – said, "This is serious.
Look at the stuff you used to do;
Sorry, lad, no room for you."

…/

So, sad, head bent, in deep disgrace
He crestfell to the Other Place
Where rapid grew his fear immortal,
Satan himself stood at the portal.
And his lieutenant, by the way,
Was, yes, you've guessed – but best not say.
When the grim pair enquired his age
His answer flung them down in rage.
"Get out. Get lost. Try Limbo, mate.
Your sins have passed their sell-by date!"

II

This dismal tale has happy sequel.
The floating spirit proved unequal
To finding satan's vague New Limbo.
Through Purgatory with limbs akimbo
He drifted to a safer shore,
The New Jerusalem's back door.
Here, smiling, Magdalena's Gardener,
The Lord, and everybody's Pardoner
Said, "Please forgive my surly mates
Who guard, by book, our Pearly Gates.
Many, turned away at first,
Feeling judged, condemned, accursed,
At last cast off their guilt and fear
And make it safe to Me, back here."

2007

Nunhead

My friend Keith Fell, a marvellous agnostic in the first
years of our friendship, died a marvellous Anglican on
29th January 1974. His passion graced both positions.
We had drunk the wine together. He is still missed.

This evening, Lord, I am content,
And if, as I tell you, I seem a little sad,
Well, blame the wine we drank;
For that too, my thanks.

The sky so clear and blue
Denies the troubled hours ahead.
It calms my soul, it stirs deep joys
And softly lights the past.

Nunhead and Lewisham, the winter trains,
Those water ices from the little shop,
Caruso records, donuts, cakes and tea
Pin-pointing Tuesday evenings in my mind.

Are these less real than present cares and fears,
Than office politics and crushing tasks?
Are dead men less than those alive today?
Are dead or living more than men to come?

"Preposterous," declares
The world's old turning Christmas face.
Dear Keith! I told him, Lord,
That nothing circumscribes your resurrection.

1971/1977

Rod and Rock

How easily, easily girls can arouse us
When our heart's in our mouth and our brain's
    in our trousers.
And there, despite the grace of God,
Went sometime I when ruled by rod.
Yet, still, with things to come in sight
I will to live and love aright.
Found, Chapter 51, Isaiah,
God's promise nigh: God's judgment nigher.
The Rock of Age, of Abraham,
Hewn from the same I know I am.

2007

The Scottish Poem

Pray God no pow'r will ever gie me
   True sight o' me as others see me.
    The Day of Judgment's nigh enough,
    I'll wait till then for a' that stuff.

2006

Scents and Sensibility

Make me blind
That no beauty later
Than yours, false seeming greater
Steal my eye.

Make me deaf
That no music after
Your voice, no other laughter
Guile my ear.

Make me dumb
That no pledge tomorrow
Elsewhere, to bring you sorrow,
Slip my tongue.

Guard my breath
That no perfume flagrant,
Fragrant but vagrant,
Bewitch me.

Chain my love
That no touch should ever
Betray you, no kiss sever
Our one flesh.

1977/2006

The 'Thank you' Our Father

Thank you, Father of us all in Heaven,
Thank you for giving us your name to hallow.
Thank you for the promise of your kingdom
And for the working of your will in this world
    as in the next.

Thank you for the daily bread
With which you have sustained us all these days
And for enabling us to forgive those who have hurt us
Just as you have forgiven us for all our offences against
    each other.
Thank you for strengthening us against temptation
And for delivering us from evil.

Thank you for the sure promise of your kingdom,
For the unfaltering exercise of your power
And for the certain hope
That we shall dwell with you in glory forever.
Amen.

2001

Vigil

"Jesus Christ, up on the cross,
Come down and show them who's the boss."
"Sorry, son, that's not my way.
Wait here, by me, until my day."

1978

Advice to a son

***Love is the heart's first ornament and the
soul's last armament***

When you were born, James, I was already a scribbler in the public prints and I wrote a public welcome to you, "Firstborn", in a northern newspaper (*reproduced on p46 of this book*). You were our first and last-born, as it turned out.

As I draw these thoughts together your mother and I are getting ready to fly out to Italy for the baptism of your own firstborn, Joseph Alessandro, a very young American on his first trip home to Europe. A good time to think about the things a father might tell his son.

Over the years I have written bits of "Advice to a Son" into the front blank leaves of our Bible and I am setting out a selection of them here, with some fuller thoughts, and sharing them with you, as indeed with all our friends in St Anthony's family.

Search your scriptures
If you and your little family can build the habit of reading just a few verses, each day or when you can, from the Old and New Testaments, you will draw deep and constant nourishment from them. Two things in particular will strike you. First, by whatever system you read you will find that again and again the New Testament will overlay and affirm what you will just have read in the Old. Second you will find that what you read comes as counsel, or warning and comfort in the precise circumstances of your life. But beware zealots ablaze with sacred texts chosen to match their obsessions as well as those who treat the Bible as a sort of raffle and stick a pin in a random page to force an answer from it. I am pointing you rather to a steady, patient and serious attention.

Suffer fools gladly
You will yourself be foolish on certain days or at certain times and you will be glad of any mercy then shown to you. I am told that when you read in someone's obituary that "He didn't suffer fools gladly" what it really means is that "he was a cantankerous old so-and-so".

Do not add to the difficulties of someone poorer than yourself

It may be that justice allows and custom encourages you to claim or reclaim something due to you from someone in harder case than yourself. But apply this principle which is part of love's higher law. Love is the heart's first ornament and the soul's last armament. You will never lose by waiting or by writing off the obligation altogether. My own father taught me this. I pass it on , confirmed by life. Your mother and I have found over the years that this is not only true but true tenfold. Whenever we have been generous we have always straight away had greater generosity showered upon us. Indeed we sometimes suspect our own motives when we give, the returns are so foolproof! The only goods we shall take out of this world with us are the goods we gave away.

Go where it's worst and do your best

I have to say that this is a counsel which I know to be noble but which, in general, my own life has not demonstrated. It may be too late but one never knows. It is the counsel which takes good teachers into tough schools and neighbourhoods. It is the counsel that draws our best young women into nursing. It is the counsel that leads young men and women to serve the poorest of the poor all round the world in the garments of Christ. It is the counsel which took James Mawdesley into the beast darkness of Burma. It is a counsel that the madding crowd despises and to which governments and corporations pay only lip service. "We're all out for ourselves really," a quite good woman said to me at work years ago. My observation has been that the best people are not.

You have already done better than I by this guidepost. I think of your student days as a cleaner in the wards of disturbed geriatrics in our local hospital. Remember old Trev from the 1914-18 war? You did well.

This is God's world; we have no business despairing of it

The encircling gloom we encounter, politically, ecologically, morally, can make our hearts sink within us, but call to mind this great fact and courage will come. If we may not despair of the world still less dare we despair of any man or woman, each one equally the triumphant pinnacle of creation.

Dare We Hope that All Men be Saved? asked Hans Urs Von Balthasar in a great book that set dreary and judging hearts against him. We surely dare not believe, still less desire, that any one be lost. We make ourselves part of the Redemption when our lives reflect this hope.

Serviam
"Non serviam" (I shall not serve) is the word of the devil. Make "Serviam" yours.

Blood is thicker than water – but hard cash may prove thicker than either
I have seen the best people and the best families fall out over money. The best place to be in a quarrel about money is missing, or at the back. Fly with the doves, not the vultures.

Be sparing with promises
Keep those you make. Never promise evil; if you find you have, break that promise because God's honour is more than a man's. Renounce vendetta.

Cultivate pity
I know you prefer the word "compassion", but I think we understand the same thing, each by the term he chooses. I heard it when young, in the older form, and thus it has stayed with me. It was a line at the end of a film, its title and players long forgotten. I should only add that you should not let your compassion fail as, so it sometimes seems, a hundred hands are stretched out to you. For are not the free gifts of God, his sunlight, your daily bread, your very life renewed unfalteringly? Then in the bad times, when your own strength is truly ebbing, you will yourself find compassion.

The host receives, the guest gives
In the matter of hospitality grasp that the guest is always the giver, the host the receiver. If you ask people to your home, to your event, they are giving you their attention, their time, their care, their new clothes, their wine, their flowers. They may not know what you will offer them, whether they will be comfortable, warm enough, cool enough, whom they might meet, whether they will be happy or at ease. You do not know what better thing they might have done instead, what they gave up to attend upon you. They honour and trust you by coming. Be grateful.

Do not resign from the labours of justice in this world from an idle confidence in the justice of the next

Our humanist and agnostic friends sometimes put us to shame by their endeavours for justice. They see. They feel. They judge. They act. Numbers of benevolent reformers toiled in the past and toil today without the final hope that sustains us. Honour and support them.

Always move towards an uncomfortable truth; for beyond it may lie the comfort of grace

An example of this is when you find your mind returning again and again to a particular moment or matter in order to justify to yourself the course of action you took. This is generally a sign that you were wrong, or not so plainly right as you thought you were. Face up to that and, so far as order and good repute allow, make amends.

Honour women and children

I know already that you do. The chief quality that a man should aim at in respect to women and children is kindness. A man fails in his manhood if women and children are afraid of him, and disfigures his manhood if the women and children closest to him are afraid.

Do not give away anything that is not yours to give

I heard this good advice from Metropolitan Anthony when he spoke to us at a meeting of The Keys, The Catholic Writers' Guild, in London many years ago. His context was the teaching and tradition of the Church but this principle will guard you from unthinking surrenders in other fields too.

Remember, finally, that I value your advice too in a world where swift-running change maroons those growing older

This article first appeared in the January 2001 issue of "Messenger of Saint Anthony", published from Padua.

Nursery
Versery

The Baby from Glamis

A baby from Glamis with long, longy arms
Decided to play with the Moon,
So he stretched his arms up and he pulled
    the globe down
And he gobbled it up with his spoon.

This darkened the night so he rose at first light
Determined to haul down the Sun
But the scorched shade of Icarus,
    travelling by kite,
Told the baby it couldn't be done.

1976/2007

Black Sheep Lullaby

*Years later James told me that he used to wonder
what a yellow Jeep was.*

No more songs, James, time to go to sleep,
    You'll go to dreamland in a yellow Jeep.
      Quick goes the night-time, soon
        comes the day,
      Up you get for breakfast then it's
        time to play.

1970

Doctor Spooner's Cat

*This egregious nonsense has to appear because my son
and some other youngsters never learnt the real version.
This is all they know. Nieces sometimes quote it back to
me on their Christmas cards. I am in favour of nieces.*

Cassy put, cassy put,
Bear have you wean?
I've bun to Lyndon
To queath a scene.

Cassy put, cassy put,
Dot width ooh, yeah.
I might end a little
Frau Schunder a hare.

1950

The Dread in the Shed

There was a young fellow called Edward
Who feared that the Thing in the shed would
Spring out on his back
In a fearful attack
Hurting more than a smack on the head would.

1976

Gold Standard

Angelina's
Sometimes been a
Little bit too bold,
But today she's
No disgrace, she's
Been as good as gold.

1975

The Kings George

A fourteen-liner let us forge
About the kings whose name was George.
The German-most, but not the worst
Was, no surprise here, George I.
The next to kingship's troubles beckoned
Was, yes, you've guessed it, George II.
There followed after, as you've heard
King George III who was absurd
   – but thank you, Doctor, for your query a
    rather sad case of porphyria?
And who came next? Er, George IV?
Ah, yeth, indeed, of courth, of courth.
Now in these last two lines lets mix the
Last two Georges, V and VI.

1967

Leonard Relents

Into the village loped Leonard the leopard.
He ate up the sheep and he swallowed their shepherd.
The villagers, fearing they might soon see lots of him
Got out their shotguns and shot all the spots off him.
Leonard the leopard now slaughters
    a lot less, yes.
Leopardly sinlessness turning
    on spotlessness.

1973

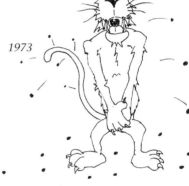

A Line of Cars

A gomley, a gomley,
Whatever is a gomley?
A gomley is a line of cars
That stretches past the Moon and stars
And comes at last to Bromley.

1970

Slaughter by Metaphor

Written for my niece Sarah on her 9th birthday

White elephants die so that parish bazaars
Can make money at Christmas, and Jaguar cars
Are constructed entirely from real jaguars
While blue bottles perish to give us blue jars.

Each bottle that's green meant, "Goodbye,
    ten green bottles"
And a hang-dog expression assuredly throttles
Some dog, whilst it's certain that crocodile tears
Mean that somewhere and sadly a croc disappears.

Marmalade's made from the marmalade cat
And cricket bats come from the cricket bat bat.
Lyons' ice cream's made from lions and that
Is as true as that rat-tails are culled from the rat.

Red herrings 'dye' in the trails of false clues
That Agatha Christie and Co like to use,
And finally, Sarah, as cruel as can be,
We drown real white horses to foam-fleck the sea.

1990

Tea for One

Upon James suggesting, at Bethersden, that the owl,
rather than setting sail with the pussy-cat, had eaten
a lion.

The owl ate a lion, he had him for tea
And after was very much bloated.
The lion's objections, I fear, went unheard
But his protest, I think, should be noted,
    be noted, be noted,
His protest, I think, should be noted.

1971

Twenty-Five-to-Four

James said he didn't like his Daddy any more
So Daddy took him up to bed, at twenty-five-to-four.
James came straight down again and made his
    Daddy roar.
So Daddy took him straight back up and this time
    closed the door.
James hammered on the door: "Daddy,
    Daddy, sorry!"
So Daddy brought him down again and promised
    him a lorry.
What kind of lorry will he buy, James Patrick
    Newman wondered.
I really think I'd rather have a new Eleven Hundred.

1970

We Can Hear Feet

We can hear feet, very small feet,
The littlest feet in the house.
It can't be a dog and it can't be a cat
And they're really too loud for a mouse.

Too soft for a horse, too firm for a mole,
How many more animal names
Shall we try as we wonder who *is* coming down?
No more, 'cos we know that it's James.

1973

Week Verse

Sunday's a fun day.
Monday's a run day.
Tuesday's a blues day.
Wednesday's a friends day.
Thursday's the worst day.
Friday's a high day
But Saturday's a flatter day.

1969

The Wiggy Waggy Woggy

There's a wiggy waggy woggy
In the biggy boggy boo,
There's a niggy naggy noggy in the noo,
There's a diggy daggy doggy
In the siggy saggy soggy,
There's a willy nilly in the bambaroo
And if you go to Haggy Hoggy
Rachel, near the taggy toggy,
You can get a cup of tea at half-past two.

2005

A Creed for a Child in 100 Words

Dear God, I believe in you.

You made everything and everyone.

I believe in Jesus, your only Son, one with you.

Because the Virgin Mary said "yes" to your Angel,

And by the Holy Spirit,

He became a man, your son and hers.

He died on the cross to save us but rose again
    as scripture said.

He ascended to your side but will return
    to judge us all.

The Holy Spirit gives life; the prophets
    spoke his words.

I adore him, as I adore you and Jesus.

I trust your Church.

I know I shall live with you forever.

1978/2007

In Grey Pavilion

Bartram

I sold this for sixpence to classmate Alan Hirst in 1947.
I owe you sixpence, Alan.

The terror of all forwards,
The man they curse and damn,
Way down in Happy Valley
We fans all call him Sam.

1947

Cowdrey

This was sent to the great man as a telegram.

Ten thousand struck you all in tons,
One hundred times one hundred runs.
We all salute such splendid stuff
But can't allow it's yet enough.
Sir, hang no boots in grey pavilion
Until your aggregate's a million.

1973

Underwood

Underwood, Underwood,
Under Milk Underwood,
Any way round the wood
Underwood knows.

Round the wood, by the wood,
Over wood, under wood,
No bat wood ever could
Get where he goes.

Miss the bat, hit the pad.
How was that? Did the lad!
Hundreds off Underwood?
Nobody can.

Flick the wood, nick the wood,
Trick-the-wood Underwood.
No batsman understood
Kent's wily man.

1970

Close of play

That last season was my leanest. I had always batted low and fielded far. I would go in at 10 or 11, then pass the rest of the afternoon at long on or long off, deep extra cover, or deep fine leg, often enough being bidden out of deep reveries to these frontier posts by the captain's shouts or semaphore.

Club records at the end of that season showed that of all members' contributions to success on the field, mine had been the most meagre. Over the whole season I amassed nine runs from five innings, an average of 1.8. There were only two ducks; on my three other visits to the middle runs accrued. My scores were one, seven, and one.

I should dwell an instant on my major innings, the seven. I had compiled three runs quite legitimately when they brought the fast man back on. He came up like a white tornado from the dark background of trees, grievous bodily harm carved into every line of him, and let fly.

Effortlessly out

I failed to get out of the way in time. The ball grazed my calf, clicking the pad strap as it sped to the pavilion. A four was signalled, entered, and stands still to my name. Straight afterwards, effortlessly, I got myself out. The record shows I never bowled. It lies. I bowled. There was a beer match following our vanquishing of a visiting team before tea. Orders are traditionally reversed for these affairs. I took an early over and clean bowled a man with my first delivery. There was a shocked hush. I apologised to the batsman as he left us, also to both captains.

Look at the record of catches taken and again my name is not there. Yet its absence conceals progress. In that season I dropped only two catches, against five the summer before.

I like to look back on that as a great upswing in my game, but in my heart of hearts I know another truth. The captain had steadily increased his skill at placing me into areas of the field unfrequented by the ball.

I rarely played the game well. At peak form I was always just a little below average. I wish I cared for it less. But boots, socks, box, sweater, flannels, all lie waiting. One never knows. I got 23 once, including a six.

This article first appeared in "The Journal",
Newcastle-upon-Tyne, on 29ᵗʰ May 1967.

About Jake Grant

Kevin's nephew Jake started drawing cartoon figures from the age of two. Educated at private and public schools in the Bournemouth area, he followed his 'A' levels with a course of study at Bournemouth Art College.

He then graduated in Illustration and Animation at Southampton Institute, where his final piece of work, a cartoon video, titled *The Stumble Inn*, was highly (though not yet widely) acclaimed. Alongside clerical work for an insurance company, Jake tries not to stress himself, although supporting Arsenal doesn't help, and he still seeks a breakthrough into the professional illustration market.

The answer to the riddle on page 76 is a candlewick.